SALISBURY

MARYLAND

SALISBURY

MARYLAND

Picturing the Crossroads of Delmarva

Dr. Gianni DeVincenti Hayes and Andy Nunez

The History Press

Published by The History Press
Charleston, SC 29403
www.historypress.net

First published 2010

Manufactured in the United States

ISBN 978.1.59629.784.5

Library of Congress Cataloging-in-Publication Data

Hayes, Gianni DeVincenti
Salisbury, Maryland : picturing the crossroads of Delmarva / Gianni DeVincenti Hayes and Andy Nunez.
p. cm.
Includes bibliographical references.
ISBN 978-1-59629-784-5
1. Salisbury (Md.)--History--Pictorial works. 2. Salisbury (Md.)--Social conditions--Pictorial works. I. Nunez, Andy. II. Title.
F189.S16D48 2009
975.2'25--dc22
2009037773

Contents

Preface

Writing histories of any place, person or event is difficult, as the only facts writers have are often the words of people who wrote about an event after it happened. The word "history" connotes the past. History can only be registered after it occurred, and with that comes the flaw of memory.

Memory is unreliable. The human brain cannot recall an event, with correct body language, proper chronology, nuances of dialogue and the description of place, without some bias. The longer time passes after an event has occurred, the more our minds inadvertently skew the truth.

Just as oral history changes with time and narrator, written history captures only what others in the past have said or written, and these often are inexact to begin with.

We have diligently worked to re-create the past for you as accurately as possible and to the best of our knowledge based on research, interviews and the work of historical societies. Not everyone will agree with us, but this book serves as a treasury of our heritage, our hopes, faith, culture, civilization and our future.

We owe a debt of gratitude through the Wicomico Historical Society to George Chevallier, highly respected historian for the city, for his time and knowledge.

Enjoy!

Acknowledgements

Thanks go to many individuals and organizations, including our families, who tried to make life easier for us while writing this book.

Special recognition goes to George Chevallier for his work and energy in helping to make this book accurate. We also thank and appreciate the following for their photos and the information they provided:

Virginia Russell Papers
Barbara Wimbrow White's Collection
The Collection of Hunter Mann III, firefighter
Executive Director Brad Bellacicco, the Salisbury Chamber of Commerce Collection
Nancy Marasco, the Poplar Hill Mansion Collection
Jason Rhodes, chair of Salisbury's 275th anniversary
Gwen Fields's Collection
Manager Jeff Korman, the Enoch Pratt Free Library Collection
Sylvia Bradley's Collection
Dr. Ray Thompson, the Collection of the Edward Nabb Research Center
Wicomico County Historical Society publications
The Hilda Fowler Collection
The Collection of Martha Graham, first female city councilwoman
The printed works of Richard W. Cooper, Charles J. Truitt, John E. Jacob and the late George Corddry

Making this book would not have been possible without their assistance and that of others.

In the Beginning

In 1598, the first European explorers sailed along present-day Worcester County, out of which Wicomico County and its seat, Salisbury, were carved in 1608. Salisbury has been and remains the principal city of the Eastern Shore.

The best words to describe Salisbury are "unprecedented growth." It developed from a handful—who sailed dangerous seas to do backbreaking work on their new homesteads—to over 30,000 (2009 estimate) and about 100,000 in the county. It transformed from vast stretches of unspoiled, vacant wilderness to one of annoying traffic congestion, large department stores and fancy restaurants. Located in the middle of the Delmarva (**Del**aware, **Mar**yland, **V**irgini**a**) Peninsula, Salisbury complements the Chesapeake Bay, which lies to the west, and features Baltimore and D.C. within a few hours' drive; together, D.C. and Baltimore have been coined the Western Shore. Philadelphia and Wilmington are to the north and Norfolk to the south. Many car decals read, "There's no life west of the Chesapeake Bay" and "Blow up the Bridge," referring to the two Chesapeake Bay bridges—the first built in 1952 and the other in 1973—that brought in hordes of urbanites who were thought to "muck up" the slow, gentle pace of shore life.

Salisbury has a rich history of old and new; natives and foreigners; sparkling sand and lush greens; water life and dirt biking; and peninsula rural and landlocked metropolis.

This "capital of Delmarva" transcended from its original sparse population to a small, throbbing city, from the "good ol' boys" days to the young, professional entrepreneurs, from majestic blue herons to annoying pigeons and from "Born Heres" to "Come Heres."

The area—"the Good Life"—is pristine in the beauty of the Chesapeake Bay and the grandeur of the Atlantic Ocean. Part of its lure is the curious original dialect of those born in the Somerset-Salisbury area—a quaint combination of a British/New England fishing village accent with a ring of a southern drawl and a creation of its own pronunciation. Mostly what are heard now are dialects from where people relocated (New York, Pittsburgh, Philadelphia, New Jersey and so on), so there are a lot of Yankee nuances.

As George H. Corddry notes in *Wicomico County History*, the flat landmass—surrounded by water on all but one side—dates back to ten to fifteen million years ago, according to fossil records. Corddry writes, "With the warming of the world climate and the melting of glaciers, which began approximately eleven hundred years ago, the sea level rose at a rate of five feet per century at first." Thus, Salisbury is referred to as a Paleochannel, which is "a vast underground reservoir of water contained in a portion of what was once a flowing river…about 150–200 ft deep. Elevation averages twenty-six feet above water level. Inhabitants of the Peninsula were predominantly Native Americans, as recorded circa 1608 by Captain John Smith—reputedly the first white person to step on the land—while exploring the Virginia/Maryland coast. He was followed by James Jones and others who came up the bay from Virginia, though they were originally from Britain and Scotland, to seek freedom of religion and fifty free acres for every man, woman and child, as mandated by Lord Baltimore.

Jones and his party met Native Americans called "Wighcocomicos" (the Wicomico tribe and the namesake of Salisbury's county), who were eventually replaced by the Pocomokes; additionally, other tribes included the Algonquins, Assateagues, Accomacks, Wetipquins, Chopticos, Chincoteagues, Transquakings, Manoakins, Yingoteagues, Naswattexes, Annamessexes, Accohannocks and Nanticokes, who were most numerous and aggressive.

Relationships between settlers and Indians were erratic; history records them as both enemies and friends. Disputes were primarily over land. The bartering staple was tobacco.

When James Jones and his party navigated their crafts up the channel, they found thick marshes, cattails, swamps, mire and forests but fertile land, too. In 1663, Jones found a clearing for the first settlement, which came to be called "Jones' Hole." His group practiced the Quaker faith. From then on, the lower shore grew into a Bible Belt passage consisting of various religions. The surnames of the pioneers of the Eastern Shore have descended to today's Salisbury residents, including Dashiell, Winder, Handy, Truitt, Smith, Elsey, Gillis, Caldwell, Woodcock, Adkins, Jackson, Disharoon, Perdue and others. Throughout its history, Salisbury's religious background grew to be a complicated one, with churches moving, changing names and taking over other churches. Yet religion remained the key to life for the settlers who created extended families and intermarried with neighbors; even today, many of the indigenous residents are related.

Their lives were rough, having to set up homesteads in the wilderness and cope with ongoing tensions from Britain, fights with the Indians, fear of wild predatory animals, struggles with taxation without representation, disasters and, over time, the Revolutionary War, the Civil War, the War of 1812, two world wars, the Great Depression and more. In the process, they engendered an American civilization of endurance, grit, perseverance and hope.

Originally, Salisbury and its county were encompassed in Somerset until one day when Isaac Handy, on his plantation at Pemberton Hall, was struck by a view that nudged him to create a commercial center at the head of the Wicomico River at Handy's Landing, thus opening the gateway to commercialism because of transportation via the Wicomico River. This center, which they called Salisbury after their beloved Salisbury, England, was founded in 1732 and incorporated in 1854. Handy's designated commercial center grew into a village, then a town and currently a bustling city with a 2009 population of over 30,000 and a metro area of about 150,000 people, while servicing a populace of approximately 350,000, thus identifying itself as the largest city and the commercial hub of all of the Eastern Shore.

The blog "Colonial Maryland" suggests that the main reason for the progress of Maryland was probably that "it had the advantage of being the first American colony that was established as a proprietorship…modeled after British Government."

Salisbury is about 11.4 square miles and lies just below the Mason-Dixon line, which essentially divided the free people from the slave labor force. Many of the slaves were given their masters' families' surnames, which live on in today's offspring in both the African American and white citizenry. Lynchings occurred but slavery began to decline from about 1820 to the end of the Civil War, when abolition was honored.

Receiving similar treatment as the slaves were Nova Scotia's French neutrals, called Acadians, who were brought into old Somerset to work the plantations. Their state of poverty and lack of understanding of the English language burdened the colonists. The government of Maryland sent aid, but over time, the Acadians disappeared, though some assimilated into the culture.

Not only were the crop plantations busy, with the Wicomico River serving as vital transportation, but Salisbury was also occupied with the battle for independence, and Maryland became the seventh state in the Union to ratify the Constitution. While Annapolis is the state capital, Salisbury has been unofficially baptized the capital of the Eastern Shore.

The city served as the axis for trade and shipping. Agriculture—the key industry of the time—grew into a giant. Strawberries, corn, oats, wheat, potatoes, fruit and tobacco were exported via ships, rail and, later, refrigerated trucks. In contrast, today, Salisbury retains some farming and a strong poultry industry, but along with these are high-tech businesses, marinas, pharmaceutical companies, shipbuilding, medicine, universities, tourism, bottling companies and a titanic retail trade surrounded by industrial parks.

The old agrarian society was complemented by the lumber business, flour mills, shirt factories, machine shops, canneries, brick and ice manufacturers and fishing; later came Perdue chickens and a hospital that has expanded to a nationally top-rated facility with more than four hundred beds.

Education emerged, not only as public schools but also as private schools and colleges.

Growth's opposite is stagnation, and this happened when the city was incorporated and certain charter elements were omitted, thus stemming development in business, government and culture. However, a bad charter and a few battles were minor compared to the major adversities that beset the area: hurricanes, blizzards, dams breaking and two catastrophic fires. Still, Salisbury towers as the hub of the shore, with its dazzling history, notable ethnic mix, landscape of water and horizon, varied and amalgamated economy, diverse industries and a social and recreational lifestyle—always with religion underpinning it.

Turn the page, relish the photos and read all about it.

Opposite: This 1926 map shows Salisbury's central location in relation to the rest of the Eastern Shore.

PHILADELPHIA
WILMINGTON
ELKTON
BALTIMORE
CHESTERTOWN
DOVER
ANNAPOLIS
WASHINGTON
CENTREVILLE
BAY
DENTON
EASTON
LEWES
REHOBOTH
GEORGETOWN
CAMBRIDGE
BAY
SALISBURY
OCEAN CITY
PRINCESS ANNE
SNOW HILL
ACCOMAC
CHESAPEAKE
EASTVILLE
ATLANTIC

This early photo postcard of Salisbury from about 1912 shows Main Street bustling with horses and buggies. A few short years would change everything. The store on the right is Lacy's Ready to Wear, owned by Lacy Thoroughgood. *George Chevallier Collection.*

Marshland along the Wicomico River provided Salisburians with ready meals of duck, muskrat and rabbits. *George Chevallier Collection.*

Slavery was prevalent around Salisbury at substantial mansions like Poplar Hill. The Underground Railroad also reputedly passed through, sending slaves north to freedom. *Library of Congress.*

Samuel P. Woodcock was a real estate developer who once operated five farms. His son donated the sixteen acres where the civic center stands, with the proviso that no alcoholic beverages be sold on the premises. Today, the civic center brings in big shows, so a debate currently rages over the need to serve alcohol to acquire high-caliber shows from all over. *Edward H. Nabb Research Center for Delmarva History and Culture at Salisbury University and the Wicomico Historical Society Collection.*

Lowe's Stables were located down near the waterfront on Dock Street and were torn down in the 1970s for a parking lot. *Edward H. Nabb Research Center for Delmarva History and Culture at Salisbury University and the Wicomico Historical Society Collection.*

Right: Here is the deaf and blind ex-slave Cyar, who served Poplar Hill in about 1900. *Poplar Hill Collection.*

Below: Said to be the oldest photo of Poplar Hill in existence, we see the 1795 mansion get its first new roof in a century. *Poplar Hill Collection.*

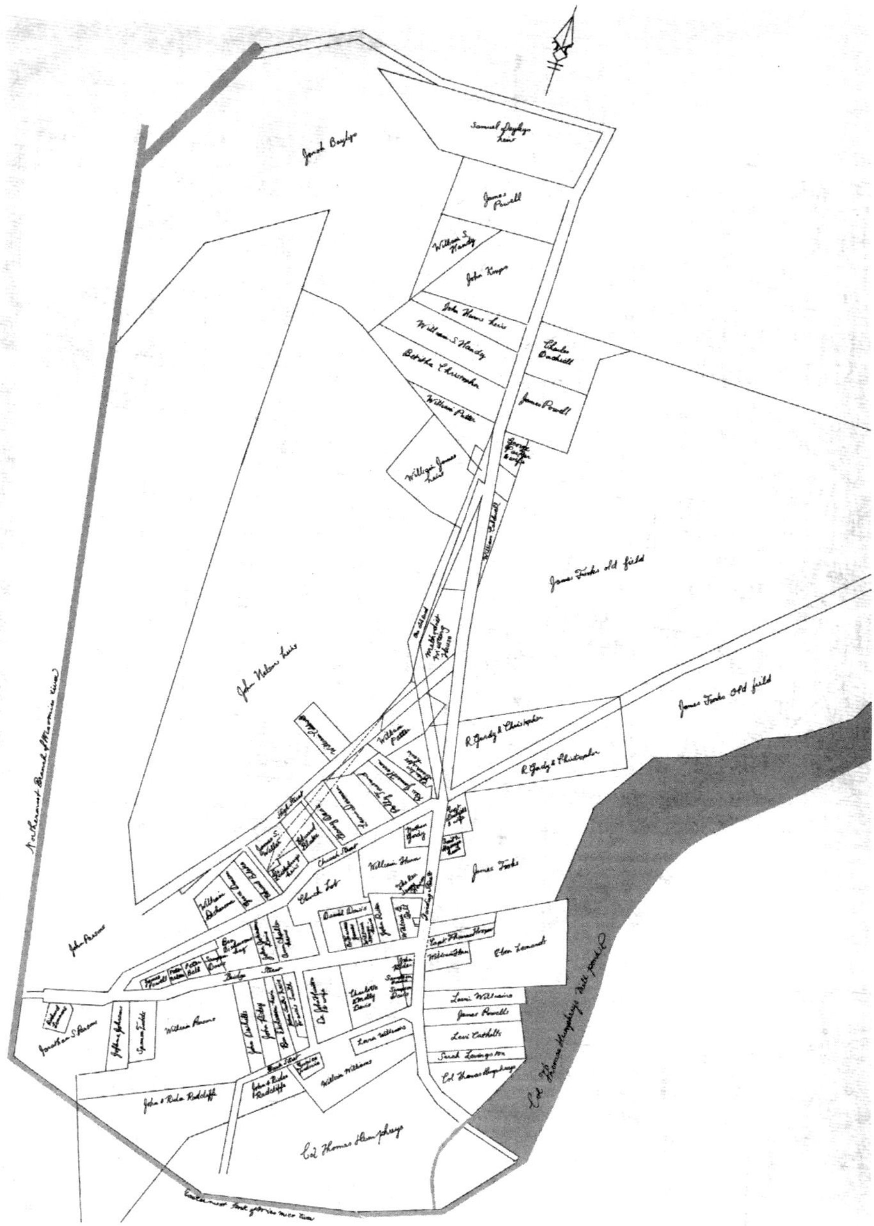

This is a reproduction of the oldest map of the city of Salisbury in existence. The original was located in the records at the Somerset County Courthouse since Wicomico County was once part of Somerset. This 1817 map shows the already steady growth of the city. *Wicomico County Historical Trust.*

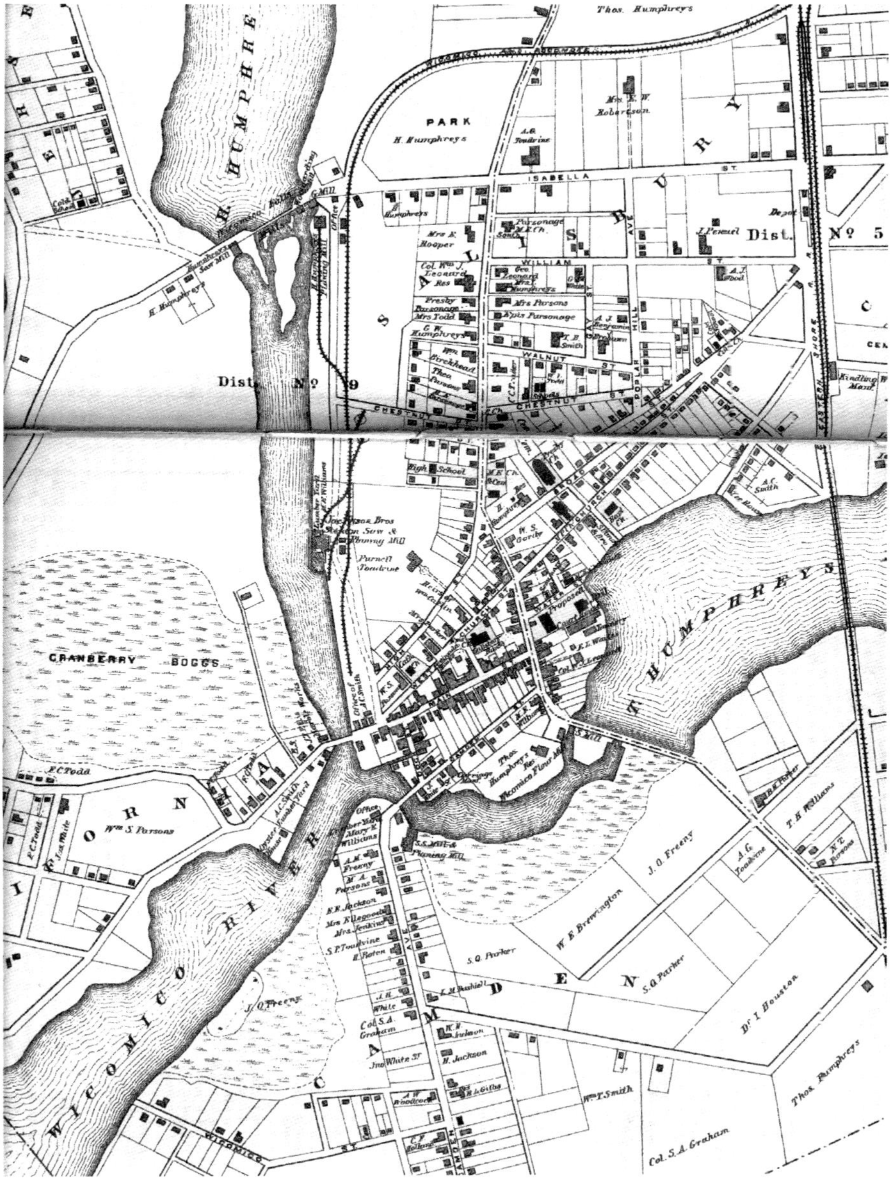

By 1877, as this map shows, Salisbury had grown tremendously, dominated by the Wicomico River and the railroad. *From the 1877* Atlas of the Eastern Shore of Maryland.

This 1937 photo depicts downtown Salisbury just a few years after the bicentennial. Taken from the courthouse lawn, the Wicomico Hotel is to the left and the Farmers and Merchants Bank is to the right. Down Division Street is the American Store. *Enoch Pratt Free Library Collection.*

The William H. Jackson House was built about 1880 and sat along Camden Avenue. Its owner was a prominent lumberman. The house burned down on September 10, 1946, and now St. Francis de Sales school sits there. *John E. Jacob Collection.*

Right: Here is the News Building, owned by the prominent Brewington family in 1908 when this photo was taken. Somewhat altered, it sits across from the courthouse on North Division Street. *Edward H. Nabb Research Center for Delmarva History and Culture at Salisbury University and the Wicomico Historical Society Collection.*

Opposite, bottom: Marion Brewington, a state senator from 1900 to 1908, was director of the Farmers and Merchants Bank and on the boards of the home for the aged and that of Peninsula General Hospital. This house still sits in the Newtown District. *Edward H. Nabb Research Center for Delmarva History and Culture at Salisbury University and the Wicomico Historical Society Collection.*

Foundation

From Bottom to Top

Salisbury ancestors endured hardships but left their mark on their descendants who picked up the shovel and built on this foundation of the early 1600s.

These pioneers had no idea that the swampy, marshy ground on which they landed was so fertile that it would spawn not only a major agrarian society but also a lifestyle. It offered a solid livelihood and trade, and the area would boost itself to the pinnacle in medical care, education, recreation and tourism.

Over the decades, the Native Americans cooperated or rebelled, depending on whom they were dealing with and what the benefits would be. In the seventeenth and eighteenth centuries, the Indians were crowded out by Anglo-Saxon settlements. If it hadn't been for a handful of settlers who braved the unfriendly terrain, the sticky humid summers and the freezing winters, who tilled land without machinery and opened businesses with no promise of patrons, Salisbury wouldn't exist today.

In 1732, residents presented a petition to the state's General Assembly to pass the Salisbury Founding Act of 1732 to form a town of fifteen acres at the head of the Wicomico River on the original land of William Winder. The designated Salisbury Town swallowed twenty acres of Handy's Landing and Pemberton's Good Will. The act passed; owners had to erect four-hundred-square-foot residences within eighteen months of purchase. Two lots sold readily, but the other eighteen didn't. The Act of 1732 had its problems, and the lots reverted to William Winder. Thirty-one years after the passing of the Founding Act of 1732, another petition requested recertification of the original act.

A few decades later, the British government removed seven thousand French settlers from Nova Scotia, of whom about nine hundred to one thousand were sent to Maryland plantations as servants, but when the Salisburians could no longer feed them, the Acadians left the Shore, though some remained and assimilated into the culture.

In 1867, Salisbury had its own county—Wicomico. Over time, both county and city grew fast. The founders and their families had planted the seeds for the small metropolis. The descendants of those founding clans are proud families, and rightly so.

Loaded and ready to go is the Gillis and Son delivery wagon, sometime after 1900. *John E. Jacob Collection.*

Opposite, top: The sales staff of the R.E. Powell store sit on the furniture delivery wagon during the first decade of the twentieth century. *John E. Jacob Collection.*

Opposite, bottom: The Charles Disharoon House was built between 1901 and 1902 and sits on the corners of Isabella and North Division Streets. Disharoon became mayor of Salisbury in 1900. *Edward H. Nabb Research Center for Delmarva History and Culture at Salisbury University and the Wicomico Historical Society Collection.*

Postmaster Marion Humphreys built this magnificent estate starting in 1904 along Camden Avenue. The rooftop balustrade and windmill in this 1908 photo are no longer part of the property, but the house still stands. *Edward H. Nabb Research Center for Delmarva History and Culture at Salisbury University and the Wicomico Historical Society Collection.*

This is the James F. Stewart Funeral Home, circa 1920. Stewart was one of the first African Americans to operate a funeral home in the area. *George Chevallier Collection.*

Senator Jesse Price was chairman of the Maryland Senate Finance Committee and as such was noted for securing funding for the first armory for Company I of the First Infantry, Maryland National Guard. This photo was taken about the time he was elected to the Maryland Senate in 1908; he later became a U.S. congressman. *Edward H. Nabb Research Center for Delmarva History and Culture at Salisbury University and the Wicomico Historical Society Collection.*

Senator Brewington was a descendant of one of the county's first families, the Breretons of Allen. He went on to become a director of the Farmers and Merchants Bank, as well as preside on the board for the hospital. This photo dates to 1908. *Edward H. Nabb Research Center for Delmarva History and Culture at Salisbury University and the Wicomico Historical Society Collection.*

This 1908 photo of the majestic W.F. Allen home on Camden Avenue was taken about four years after completion. The Allen family was famous for their agricultural products, especially strawberries. The building was torn down after the property became part of the Salisbury University complex. *Edward H. Nabb Research Center for Delmarva History and Culture at Salisbury University and the Wicomico Historical Society Collection.*

In this photo we see John Melson in the office of W.F. Messick Ice Company, founded in 1920, a prominent business located near the railway station. *Barbara Wimbrow White Collection.*

This circa 1910 photo shows the G.W.D. Waller family in front of Poplar Hill Mansion. Waller, a prominent lawyer, owned the property through the first half of the twentieth century. Pictured with him are his wife, his son Doan and daughters Carolyn and Julia. The woman in the wide-brimmed hat and the boy on the right are unknown. *Poplar Hill Collection.*

The British connection came to Salisbury in 1932 when the city celebrated its centennial. Here we see lawyer G.W.D. Waller, *center*, with Mayor J. Sidney Rambridge of Salisbury, England, on the left and Councilor Batt on the right. *Poplar Hill Collection.*

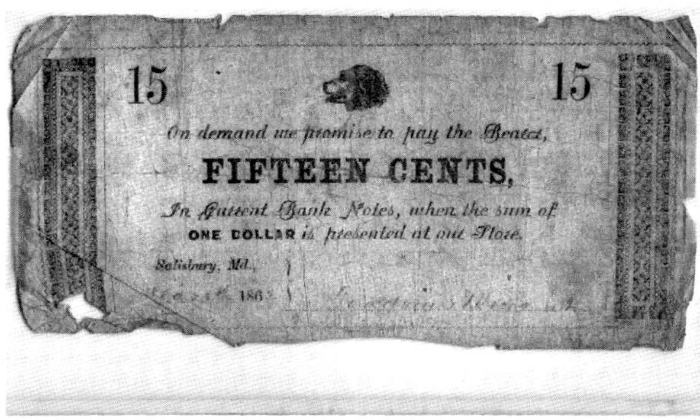

During the Civil War, there was a shortage of paper currency. Alexander Toadvine, future first mayor of Salisbury (1888–90), and his partner Thomas Vincent devised their own scrip in 1862. *George Chevallier Collection.*

This 1936 aerial shot by the National Guard shows Salisbury's growth in the seventy-one years since the Civil War and the new jail under construction behind the courthouse. *Enoch Pratt Free Library Collection.*

Company I of the Maryland National Guard spreads out in front of the courthouse about 1918. *Gwen Fields Collection.*

Here are some cheerful spectators for the Baltimore, Chesapeake and Atlantic (BC&A) Railroad train as it passes by, circa 1908. *Edward H. Nabb Research Center for Delmarva History and Culture at Salisbury University and the Wicomico Historical Society Collection.*

In this photo we see Arthur W. Perdue, founder of the company that still bears his name, on February 28, 1968, hanging the first chicken to go through the new processing plant that was built near downtown. His son Frank made the name Perdue synonymous with chicken, and Frank's son Jim—third generation—now runs the large company. *John E. Jacob Collection.*

The downtown post office building was constructed in 1925. About the time this photo was taken, 1936, murals were being painted inside as part of the Work Projects Administration (WPA) project. *Enoch Pratt Free Library Collection.*

Dedicated in 1915, this fortress-like armory building replaced the original after it was destroyed by fire in 1914. It became the headquarters for Company I of the Twenty-ninth Infantry division. *Enoch Pratt Free Library Collection.*

Another WPA project was this dam built to improve the water supply in 1937. *Enoch Pratt Free Library Collection.*

Football was an important part of high school sports during the first half of the twentieth century. Here we see the 1914 Wicomico High School football team. *Barbara Wimbrow White Collection.*

This is the 1917 Wicomico High School team. *Barbara Wimbrow White Collection.*

Horace van Auken and C. Ercell Wimbrow check voting machines for the 1966 municipal election. *Barbara Wimbrow White Collection.*

Livelihood

Land and Water

Salisbury features rich land, deep waters and blue skies. Besides working the land and water, the "Bury" populace plies the Atlantic Ocean, the Chesapeake Bay and all their tributaries to swim, motor, sail, yacht and fish. Work means tending the crops and breeding chicks to satisfy Perdue Farms, MountAire and Allen chickens. For profit today, farmers are selling their unplowed acreage to builders for housing developments and sports fields—from minor league champions to the professional Shorebirds running the diamond at Perdue Stadium. Festivals are chief recreational forums. In winter, the city park lights up with designed Christmas forms; horse and wagon rides with hot cocoa; and decorations placed throughout the entire downtown.

Fun is fun, but business is business. Chesapeake Shipbuilding is serious about erecting tugs, cruise boats and ferries and has enough work for several years. With water comes the watermen, who are a dying breed. Just as factories, canning, shirt making, mill working and forestry nosedived, transit, education, healthcare, high technology and electronics swelled as big businesses. Mom and pop inns and stores compete against four-star hotels and motels, department stores, vineyards, chain restaurants and sales and repairs, as well as the sixteen-screen multiplex theatre at the "new mall," called The Centre at Salisbury. The downtown core features government workers and all law and protective personnel, as well as the mayor, city inspectors, city council and others. Stores are few on Main Street, which has gone from a throbbing core with open streets to a closed walking plaza and back again to open streets with only one-way traffic; city residents continue to brainstorm over how to bring foot traffic back instead of competing with the malls and major national stores in the North Corridor.

Salisbury flourished into a modern city with a high-volume metro core that services over 350,000 people and functions as the medical and educational nucleus of the Shore. A major promoter of this from 1920 onward has been the Salisbury Chamber of Commerce. Nevertheless, the city weathered rough times, too, especially when work was sparse. Blacksmiths, farmers, tavern owners, merchants, weavers, commissioners, sheriffs, constables, attorneys, ferrymen, doctors, laborers/servants, millwrights, mariners, tailors, carpenters, coopers, sawyers, ministers, road/bridge builders and other occupations dotted the village. Then, in the early to mid-1800s, Salisbury championed steamships, railroads, river craft and, eventually, trucks, vans and automobiles, along with communications capabilities. The hustle and bustle was never more prominent than from the mid-1800s through the 1960s and early 1970s, when residents strolled downtown, visiting stores, chatting in bars and eateries, banking and engaging in other activities.

Nearly two thousand farms existed in 1900, which dwindled to about three hundred in 2006. Back in the early 1900s, the average farm tilled about seventy-four acres and grew oats, hay, forage, potatoes, sweet potatoes, wheat, corn, apples, figs and strawberries, along with herding thousands of cattle, horses and swine. According to the Nabb Research Center, business burgeoned, sweeping throughout the village.

Over time, trucking, railroading and the marina soared to major production status. Shops opened—from clothes to jewelry to soda and feed mills. Medical care took to the forefront with the then named Peninsula General Hospital (PGH), founded in 1897. Education blossomed, with the founding of the Salisbury Normal School, which later became Salisbury University with about eight thousand students. Wor-Wic College helped educate a boatload of traditional and adult students, with a campus located on the east side of Salisbury.

While the pioneers are credited for sculpting and shaping the city, their descendants fine-tuned it into the highly defined livelihood nexus that it is today.

For many, then, Salisbury is the golden city—the gem—of the Peninsula.

In 1890, Dean Perdue and Somers Gunby had been selling carriages since 1881 at this location near Market Street. Today, it is a section of the municipal parking lot. *John E. Jacob Collection.*

Bob Toulson was a young, enterprising African American and operated several businesses from his tiny building on Church Street. He and his wife Cecie shined shoes, pressed clothes and helped out folks oppressed by Prohibition. The building site is now located under the road (U.S. Route 13). *John E. Jacob Collection.*

Charles Ulman's store was located on the ground floor of the Ulman Opera House in 1905. It carried numerous items, including many Christmas toys. *John E. Jacob Collection.*

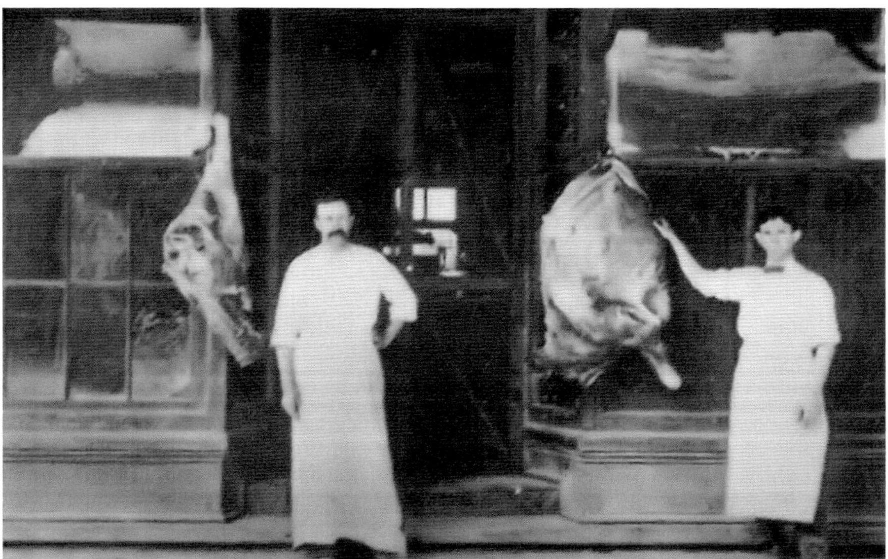

L.S. Short had a butcher shop along Dock Street, later known as Market Street; in 1908 he displayed the quality of his establishment. *John E. Jacob Collection.*

Charles Ralph started a decades-long tradition of selling fine men's clothing from a shop on Main Street in the 1920s, later merging with Clement Gaskill. *John E. Jacob Collection.*

The Merchant Hotel sat at the convergence of Main and Church Streets. Built in 1888, it was a short-lived affair and was bought by the Johnson Candy Company. *John E. Jacob Collection.*

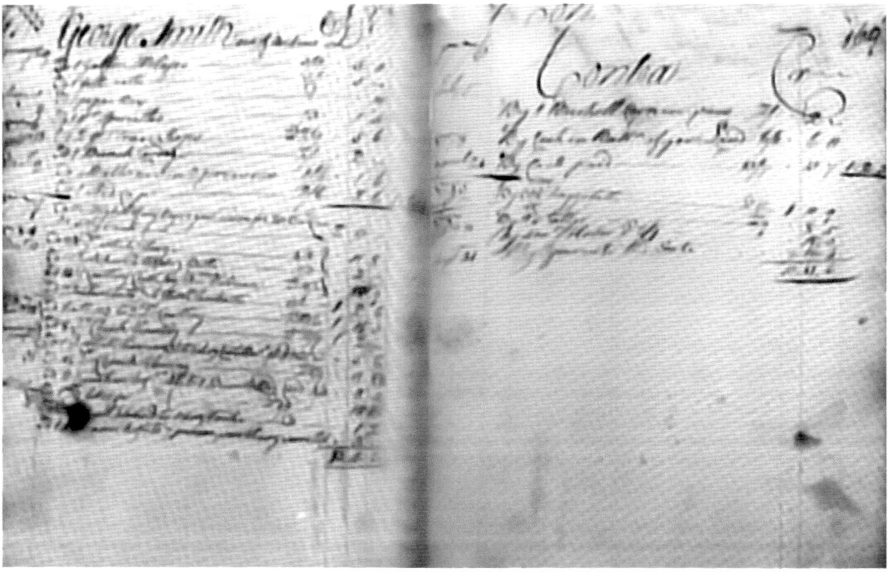

Salisbury was founded as a center of commerce, as demonstrated by the 1775 entries of storekeeper John Nelms. *John E. Jacob Collection.*

In 1921, Salisbury's police force consisted of six individuals—including the chief! Now it has over one hundred officers and staff and continues to grow. *John E. Jacob Collection.*

The city hall doubled as the fire hall for a time, as seen in this 1908 photo. The tower was built to a specific height so fire hoses could be hung down to dry. The building now belongs to the adjacent St. Peter's Episcopal Church. *Edward H. Nabb Research Center for Delmarva History and Culture at Salisbury University and the Wicomico Historical Society Collection.*

Homer E. White's shoe store, shown here in this 1908 photo, stood along the western end of Main Street; its most memorable feature was its giant shoe fixture. *Edward H. Nabb Research Center for Delmarva History and Culture at Salisbury University and the Wicomico Historical Society Collection.*

The repair and installation crew of Diamond State Telephone Company took time out from their exploding business in Salisbury to pose for this 1908 photograph showing the latest models. *John E. Jacob Collection.*

This plaque comes from the side of the current courthouse and declares that up until the last half of the 1800s, the area was the site of the historic Byrd Tavern, a favored place for travelers. John Byrd, its proprietor, was killed following an argument during the Civil War when the city was under occupation by Union troops. *John E. Jacob Collection.*

Salisbury, England's Mayor Sidney Rambridge arrives at the courthouse in full regalia during the 1932 celebration of Salisbury's bicentennial. *Poplar Hill Collection.*

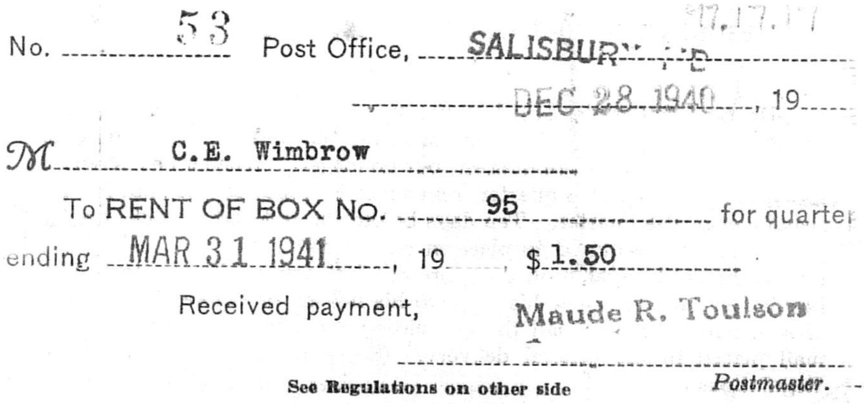

No. 53 Post Office, SALISBUR

DEC 28 1940, 19

M C.E. Wimbrow

To RENT OF BOX No. 95 for quarter

ending MAR 31 1941, 19 , $1.50

Received payment, Maude R. Toulson

See Regulations on other side Postmaster.

Here is a receipt to C. Ercell Wimbrow signed by Maude R. Toulson, postmistress of Salisbury in 1941. The post office was renamed the Maude Toulson Federal Building in her honor. *Barbara Wimbrow White Collection.*

James Lank stands by the workstation he occupied for over half a century as an employee of Grier Machine Shop. He started in 1896 and is shown here in 1952. *Barbara Wimbrow White Collection.*

Opposite, top: This nineteenth-century jail was replaced in 1936. Note the lack of bars in the windows. *George Chevallier Collection.*

Opposite, bottom: In 1936, the courthouse had been standing for almost sixty years and recently had been remodeled by the addition of a new jail wing to replace the smaller version. *Enoch Pratt Free Library Collection.*

COURT HOUSE SALISBURY, MD.

An important icon along Lake Street was the James Weatherly's Postal Card shop. It was a prime gathering spot for the African American community of Salisbury; its meeting hall was upstairs. *George Chevallier Collection.*

Tom Cimino came to America from Italy and shortened his family name to Cinno. In the 1920s, he opened Cinno's Confectionary, which became a favorite hangout from the 1920s to the 1940s. From the left are his sons Leonard and Sam, with Tom on the right. *George Chevallier Collection.*

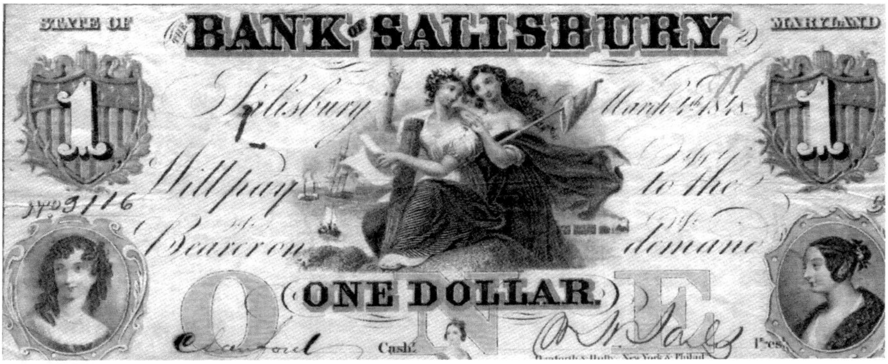

Salisbury changed from barter and state-printed scrip supplemented by Spanish silver to bank-backed currency like this 1848 one-dollar note from the Bank of Salisbury, which sat on Main Street near where WMDT-TV 47 is now located. *George Chevallier Collection.*

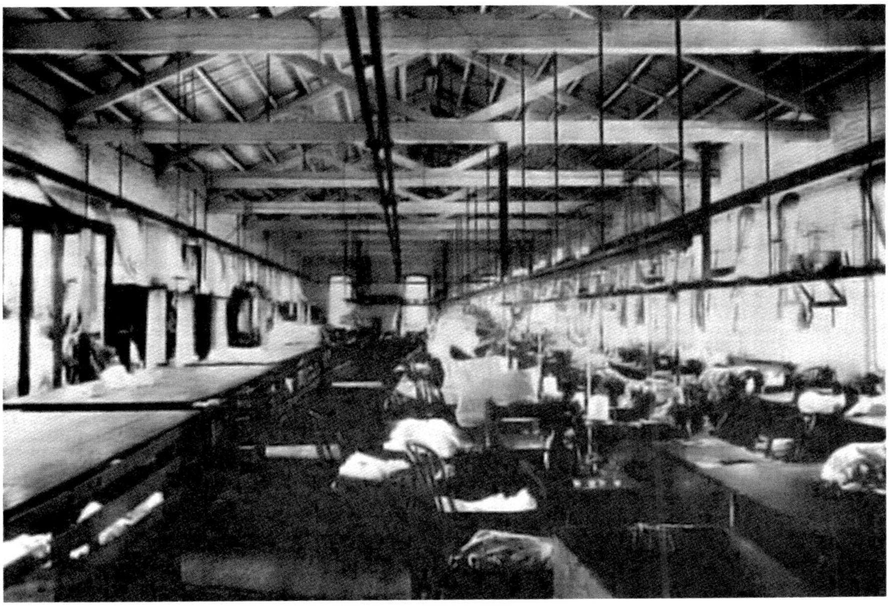

The Jackson Gutman shirt factory was established in 1897, and at its height it employed nearly four hundred people at its colossal facility, but eventually it went bankrupt. *John E. Jacob Collection.*

Left: The Wicomico Hotel was a downtown icon for nearly half a century after its completion in 1924. It is now a suite of office buildings located across the street from the courthouse. *Martha Graham Collection.*

Below: The Oaks Drive-in was another memorable spot, shown here during the 1960s. *George Chevallier Collection.*

This advertising artwork shows the modern Salisbury Chamber of Commerce building as it looked in the 1960s. *Salisbury Chamber of Commerce Collection.*

Frank Perdue, the symbol of the poultry industry on the Delmarva Peninsula, used this classic ad from the 1970s. *Salisbury Chamber of Commerce Collection.*

The Wicomico Library occupied several buildings around town until it settled on the old armory property on North Division Street and was given a face-lift. It now seeks to build an even larger library downtown to accommodate the growing population. *John E. Jacob Collection.*

Oliphant Chevrolet along with Cavanaugh Ford were the top two car dealerships in Salisbury after World War II. Oliphant's iconic Ollie the Elephant was featured in ads for decades. *George Chevallier Collection.*

C. Ercell Wimbrow poses with the alumni of the Wicomico High School class of 1917 in this 1967 photo of their fiftieth reunion. He is in the back row, standing fourth from left. *Barbara Wimbrow White Collection.*

This 1958 grand jury photo is unique because it marked the first time that women were seated on the grand jury of Wicomico County. *John E. Jacob Collection.*

The year 1992 marked another first as Martha Graham was sworn in as the first female city council member. *Martha Graham Collection.*

Martha Graham soon learned the duties of politics as she is seen here during a chicken-plucking contest competing against the future State of Maryland Secretary of Agriculture Lewis Riley. *Martha Graham Collection.*

James English began his restaurant career in 1933 using the motif of a silver dining car. The business expanded over the years and is now but a fond memory. *Salisbury Chamber of Commerce Collection.*

Johnny Testa and Sammy Cerniglia created one of Salisbury's legendary restaurants in 1946, downtown on Route 13. It soon became the top dining and entertainment spot in Salisbury, with live music featured at its posh Alpine Room. *Salisbury Chamber of Commerce Collection.*

In 1968, Salisbury saw the opening of its first mall. The eighty-acre site became a relocation magnet for stores from all parts of the city, but its fate would change twenty-two years later. *George Chevallier Collection.*

Situated on North Route 13, Salisbury Pewter was a haven for gifts and utensils for several decades. Now in a new location, it manufactures gift and commemorative pieces that are used by the White House as gifts for dignitaries and visiting heads of state, including the delivery of a sterling frame that was presented to the Crown Prince and Princess of Denmark in 2009. Here it is seen in full Christmas regalia sometime in the 1970s. *Authors' Collection.*

Industry

Light and Heavy

The colonists, upon arriving at the marshland via primordial watercraft, saw their livelihoods to be primarily those of fishing and farming. But over time, jobs sprouted in various other sectors: tree farms and lumber industry, sawmills, flour mills, rail, steamships, blacksmithing, foundry work, canning, machining and the making of gas pumps by Wayne Dresser—one of the first major industries in Salisbury—as well as cork and bottling, medical care and heavy-duty and light manufacturing. During the peaceful years with the Indians, the settlers learned about planting and caring for crops and cattle, which in turn prompted a transportation industry to spawn on the Wicomico River. The early settlers accommodated military equipment and quartered soldiers through the wars. The Anthony Johnson family, planters, proved to be the initiators of successful black businesses even in the grip of slavery.

From the area's nascence, seafood became a major livelihood, as did the labor-intensive killing/cleaning production of seafood and chickens. Perdue's world headquarters thrives in Salisbury. The trucking and shipping industry took off, too. Later, different types of occupations emerged, such as automotive work, pewter manufacturing, airport jobs, secondary education, high-tech companies, manufacturing and assembling factories and pharmaceutical companies, along with the electronic components business and all types of fiber and computerization jobs and top-shelf medical care.

The major employers in the city now are Peninsula Regional Medical Center, Salisbury University, Wor-Wic College, city government, Perdue Farms (with a total employment greater than the population of the city of Salisbury) and the Salisbury Board of Education and its employees, according to online statistical sources.

Other chief employers, both in the past and in the burgeoning present, include Verizon, Campbell Soup, Pepsi Bottling, Harvard Custom Manufacturing, Sharp Water, USAir/Piedmont Airlines, Perdue Stadium and its Shorebirds baseball franchise, government and protective services and a pulsing, vibrant tourist industry with numerous parks and playgrounds enhancing the city. Enriching the metro area are class A lodging and restaurants; city and county marinas; Ward Wildfowl Art exhibits; various museums; cultural, musical and historical places; NavTrak; Toroid Corporation; MaTech; K&L Microwave; newspapers; radio networks; television stations; and magazines, along with various associations and organizations, Super Walmarts, Sam's and other retail outlets.

All of these contemporary stores have made Salisbury a hustling, lively city where traffic clogs arteries and lines queue up for long periods.

Left: A good deal of the area down by the river was a vast cranberry bog, but the need for more commercial land won out. It would become the Grant Shopping Center. *John E. Jacob Collection.*

Below: The Grier brothers, Fred and Robert, went into business in 1888 but parted ways in 1903. This machine shop, later known as R.D. Grier and Company, remains a fixture of Salisbury life. *John E. Jacob Collection.*

From humble beginnings sprang a mighty empire. Here is the Arthur Perdue hatchery built in 1925. Now Perdue products span the globe. *John E. Jacob Collection.*

Another trackside business was the W.T. Banks bottling company, which turned out several flavors of soda. This 1908 photo shows kids lined up for refreshment. *Edward H. Nabb Research Center for Delmarva History and Culture at Salisbury University and the Wicomico Historical Society Collection.*

The L.W. Gunby Company built this warehouse for its hardware business in its heyday in 1908. *Edward H. Nabb Research Center for Delmarva History and Culture at Salisbury University and the Wicomico Historical Society Collection.*

The Tilghman Fertilizer Company sat well away from most businesses and residences along the Wicomico River, as seen in this aerial shot from 1936. Note the city's name on the roof along with a directional indicator. *Enoch Pratt Free Library Collection.*

Here are four 1908 views of the E.S. Adkins Lumber company that was a fixture on North Salisbury Boulevard until it closed a few years back. *Edward H. Nabb Research Center for Delmarva History and Culture at Salisbury University and the Wicomico Historical Society Collection.*

The Salisbury Candy Company, seen here in 1908, distributed candy from several manufacturers. *Edward H. Nabb Research Center for Delmarva History and Culture at Salisbury University and the Wicomico Historical Society Collection.*

Known collectively as the Manhattan building, the rear of this long complex along Main Street was the Manhattan Shirt Factory, while the storefronts, as seen in this 1936 photo, held a variety of shops, including a drugstore. Today it still houses small businesses and a restaurant. *Enoch Pratt Free Library Collection.*

This turn-of-the-twentieth-century photo shows the schooner *J.S. Hoskins* delivering cedar shingles from Florida to the Tilghman Company. *Poplar Hill Collection.*

By 1908, the Peninsula Brick Company had been situated along the tracks for many years. *Edward H. Nabb Research Center for Delmarva History and Culture at Salisbury University and the Wicomico Historical Society Collection.*

This old photo shows the long-departed Webb Packing Company on Truitt Street.
George Chevallier Collection.

Several employees at Wayne Pump admire the new "Blended Fuel" gas pump in 1956.
George Chevallier Collection.

Lifestyle and Culture

The "Born Heres" and the "Come Heres"

The homesteaders in Salisbury had no idea how coarse and tough life could get on overgrown land and forests. Average age of death was forty-three.

They were awed by the great blue herons, snow white egrets, mergansers, Canada geese, mallard ducks, swans, bald eagles, orioles and abundant deer, along with feral mammals, endless water life (shellfish, rockfish, menhaden, terrapin, marlin, crabs, tuna, tortoises) and large, multi-varied trees and plants. Locally noted historian Richard Cooper states in *Portrait of Salisbury, Maryland through the 1900s* that "the area we live in was but a short while ago nothing but pure wilderness, inhabited by people who had hardly advanced beyond the Stone Age culture. Those who ventured here were actually less prepared for what existed here than the astronauts who landed on the moon."

The blog "Colonial Maryland" states that there were "few landowners in [all of] Colonial Maryland. Those who did own land were almost all Catholic. Most of the workers, conversely, were Protestant indentured servants. In no other colony, and certainly not in England itself, were Catholics at the top of the social and economic hierarchy." Landowners kept busy working, stopping only to converse with others on farming methods, keeping law and order and being involved in local government. Most troublesome was communication; it could take a fortnight to get a reply to a message. Hence, most business transactions took weeks to complete.

The outdoors was the man's domain, and many men had equipment parts and tools lying around since they had to perform their own repairs. Agriculture, marketing and retail jobs expanded.

There were three women to every man, and they were slightly older. Female settlers in Maryland had greater social power than did their counterparts in England, according to the "Colonial Maryland" blog.

A woman had to be sturdy to cross the sea (many managing the ocean fare by serving as five-year indentured servants to households). Whether handmaid or wife, her primary domain was the home, with all of its chores and none of the modern conveniences. With no refrigerator, food had to be prepared from scratch daily and entirely eaten to avoid waste. Women churned cream into butter, sewed, nourished and washed children, homeschooled older kids, fed chickens, milked cows, gardened and picked tobacco, taught religion (Quakerism) and made families go to homes at which scripture was read and discussed. The women also played doctor and mitigated everyone's emotional and physical ills.

The first taste of professional medicine was through herbalists. Later came a few country-style doctors and then a clinic; next was a small infirmary called Peninsula General Hospital, a "112-year-old institution" that grew into a giant hospital/trauma center, according to the Peninsula Regional Medical Center website.

Homes were only one-room or two-room log cabin types, heated by burning fires that also served as the cooking element. Early homes had no insulation, so freezing air seeped in during the rare icy, snowy weather, and nor'easters and hurricane winds cut right through the walls.

Alcohol was used as both a relaxant and a way to escape the rugged life. Moonshiners operated the alcohol trade even during Prohibition. Ordinances were slapped on homeowners; sheriffs, mayors and other legal and political bodies enforced them. Crime ratcheted up from spats with the Indians, with colonists shooting them and the Indians in turn slaying settlers. Soon the Native Americans retreated to Delaware—the first state to ratify the Constitution (Maryland was the seventh).

Extended groups—families, friends and neighbors—interacted for safety, assistance, work and convenience. They rose at dawn and went to bed with the first hint of dusk. They recreated in "beautiful natural areas [to] enjoy activities such as boating, swimming, fishing, bird watching," according to Rachel Cooper's article "Maryland's Eastern Shore." To their benefit, their lifestyle improved when the Industrial Revolution roared in.

Even today, there is a sense of ownership of Salisbury by those families born and raised here, who refer to themselves as the "Been Heres" or "Born Heres" (those new to the area, even if residing in Salisbury for decades, are called the "Come Heres"). Both sides present a running feud in the daily newspaper, making the issue legendary and comedic. From time to time, Peninsula residents have proposed to secede from their respective states and form a new state called Delmarva. Legislation has been submitted to the Maryland General Assembly three times for this purpose, most recently in 1998. The online guide "Eastern North Carolina, Virginia and Maryland" has more information on this topic and others.

Throughout the decades, Salisburians enriched their lives with the arts, a zoo, symphony, museums—especially the famous Ward Museum of Wildfowl Art—the Edward H. Nabb Research Center and Pemberton Hall, along with all of the culture and intellectual enlightenment provided by surrounding colleges.

Carolyn Waller, daughter of prominent lawyer G.W.D. Waller, was fortunate enough to become queen of the Bicentennial Celebration of 1932; she is seen here in full regalia. *Poplar Hill Collection.*

Temperance committees came out in force well before Prohibition became law, and in this 1922 photo, the results of a successful raid on illegal moonshiners are displayed. *John E. Jacob Collection.*

In 1921, the *Wicomico News* had been turning out quality papers for several decades after Harry and Marion Brewington bought the building that sits on the corner of Main and North Division Streets, though slightly altered today. *John E. Jacob Collection.*

Salisbury had been a center for the arts for over a century when this mid-twentieth-century photo was taken of the Salisbury Symphony Orchestra, which is still going strong today. *Salisbury Chamber of Commerce Collection.*

During the Great Depression, the federal government sponsored several public works projects, including painting murals at the downtown branch of the post office. Completed in 1935, they depicted scenes of Salisbury history, including this scene from its steamboat days. *Enoch Pratt Free Library Collection.*

Opposite, bottom: Another fixture on North Division Street is the Scottish Rite Masonic Lodge. In this 1978 photo, Sovereign Grand Inspector General of Maryland Masons John Donaldson (first row, left) bestows honors on fifty-year members from the Salisbury lodge. The only fellow not wearing a cap is C. Ercell Wimbrow. *Barbara Wimbrow White Collection.*

Here is a rare item, the cover of the 1913 Wicomico High School literary magazine. *The Ides* contained prose and poetry from students. *Gwen Fields Collection.*

In 1896, baseball was a popular sport in Salisbury. This photo of the Salisbury Base Ball Club [*sic*] was taken at the ball field on Fairground Drive where Pemberton Apartments now sit. *John E. Jacob Collection.*

This 1956 photo shows the Pony League Park. The old Salisbury Mall property covers it now. *George Chevallier Collection.*

The firemen's muster was a staple for the fire departments from all over the area. Usually held at the city park, hundreds would compete for trophies in friendly competition. This photo was taken before World War II. *Hunter Mann III Collection.*

Besides sports, kids followed the simpler pleasures of the early twentieth century. Here we see young Doan Waller transporting his sister Carolyn out in front of Poplar Hill Mansion, circa 1910. *Poplar Hill Collection.*

The Community Players were formed in 1936 and are still in existence, having gained a reputation around the peninsula as professional stage staff and actors. This photo was taken in 1958. *John E. Jacob Collection.*

Fox hunting was popular, and the Wicomico Hunt Club was formed in 1929, remaining a fixture of Salisbury society for decades afterward, as shown by this 1965 photo. *John E. Jacob Collection.*

Television came to Salisbury in 1954 with CBS station WBOC. This 1962 photo shows a filming of the Jaycees-sponsored Miss Maryland contest. The studio has recently undergone a large addition. *John E. Jacob Collection.*

Tennis became a popular sport and remains a staple of Salisbury athletic life. Here we see former tennis great Jimmy Connors competing in Salisbury in 1973. *John E. Jacob Collection.*

The City Park, established during the Depression years, is marked by a meandering stream that attracts fishermen young and old, as evidenced by this diverse crowd from the latter half of the twentieth century as they vie for awards in a fishing contest. The park boasts summer concerts, paddle-boating, Christmas community get-togethers and "sleigh" rides, as well as the ever-popular zoo. *Wicomico County Historical Society Collection.*

The Wicomico and Nanticoke Rivers once teemed with striped bass, known as rockfish, as seen in this vintage photo showing the massive size of a "roller." *Wicomico County Historical Society Collection.*

This photo from the latter half of the twentieth century shows preparation for a church dinner featuring muskrat, once prized for its hide and still found as a delicacy in Salisbury though smaller than the turkey in the photo. *Wicomico County Historical Society Collection.*

In May 1968, the tragic shooting of an African American deaf-mute by Salisbury police after he failed to respond to an order to stop caused racial problems to boil over as a knot of protesters gathered outside the police station, calling for punishment of the officer. *John E. Jacob Collection.*

The racial problems grew even more violent when young African Americans, feeling discontent over perceived injustice in the May shooting, destroyed two white-owned stores in their neighborhood. It took the combined efforts of the Maryland State Police and National Guard to quell tensions. *John E. Jacob Collection.*

Here are the Salisbury Zoo's spectacled bears in 1977. This and many other exhibits are still shown there, like buffalo, alligators and llamas. *Authors' Collection.*

The Delmarva Chicken Festival remains one of the area's largest gatherings and has been hosted by Salisbury several times. In this photo, workers turn a metal basket holding several dozen chickens. *John E. Jacob Collection.*

The Chicken Festival, begun in 1948, soon featured the "World's Largest Frying Pan." The pan was ten feet in diameter and had an eight-foot handle. It weighed 650 pounds and could hold eight hundred chicken quarters. *John E. Jacob Collection.*

This 1947 snapshot of a Brownie troop was taken by a proud mother where St. Francis de Sales Catholic School is today. *George Chevallier Collection.*

The Ward Museum of Wildlife Art was established in 1968 to honor the champion wildfowl carvers Lem and Steve Ward. Since 2000, it has been an affiliated foundation of Salisbury University. *Authors' Collection.*

The Bury Celebrates

The city basks in festivals and parades, nationally recognized tournaments, symphonies, art—both fine and literary—drama and theatre, hunting and fishing, sports and university activities. It boasts of group and individual donations to the needy and to charities, and philanthropists build halls, classrooms and sports stadiums.

Salisbury also crows about being in the nation's top ten for its small zoo, parks, cultural centers, areas of historical exploration and the main library and its satellites, as well as being proud of Pemberton Historical Park and other events like wine fests, turtle races and food contests. Entertainment was important to the hardworking colonists.

The Waller family knew a lot about entertaining and celebrating. G.W.D. Waller was a prominent lawyer who bought Poplar Hill Mansion, the oldest house inside the city limits, in 1897. He and his wife raised Doan, Carolyn and Julia, and they lived at the mansion until after World War II. Doan became a naval officer and taught cadets until his untimely death in 1946. Carolyn and Julia each married and moved away. But Carolyn returned and participated in the 250th anniversary in 1982, picked from a number of entrants to be queen of the Bicentennial Celebration of 1932. Guests of honor included the mayor of Salisbury, England, Sidney Rambridge, as well as Maryland's Governor Albert Ritchie. The airship *Akron* flew over the city. The parade started on Fitzwater Street and ended five hours later where the current civic center now stands. Endless elaborate floats glided down the streets packed with spectators. The grand march of dignitaries and Carolyn's coronation meshed in a symphony of remembrance, fun, food and honor.

Salisbury's Wicomico County was incorporated in 1867; the 1967 centennial rolled in with a loud bang. Like the bicentennial, the city's centennial hoopla lasted a full week, with lots of activities: movies, music and speeches. Numerous plays and performances and mock events—such as kangaroo courts—went on, as did promenades by the Centennial Belles in period dress.

Important people and high-level visitors caravanned throughout the city. After attending the celebration, more "Come Heres" arrived who talked and moved fast, had Yankee accents and wanted everything on the spot right away.

The metro area jumps on any reason to celebrate. The Salisbury Festival lasts one weekend, and something happens in every nook and cranny of downtown; the Chicken Festival shows off its mammoth frying pan and basket for chicken; Pork in the Park garners huge attention; and Christmastime is busy daily with holiday events.

In 2007, Salisbury had its 275th anniversary feast, but such special occasions aren't the only times when the residents kick up their heels. They do so in honor of or in memory of others and for charitable causes, as the city and county embrace some of the most giving people.

Here we see some folks at the 1896 Fireman's Bazaar, held on Lemon Hill, where Parsons Home now sits. *John E. Jacob Collection.*

The 1932 Salisbury Bicentennial celebration went on for one week and featured a grand parade down Main Street. The local fire department, with young and old members, joined in the march past the courthouse. *Poplar Hill Collection.*

The year 1912 saw the election of Woodrow Wilson as president, delighting the mostly Democratic members of Salisbury. They put together an impromptu parade of their own, complete with flag-draped carts. *George Chevallier Collection.*

Shown in 1934 and parked in front of what is now Wicomico Middle School near the city park is President Franklin Delano Roosevelt, in town to drum up support for a local senatorial candidate. *John E. Jacob Collection.*

Many dignitaries, including Governor Albert Ritchie, packed the reviewing stand along with the mayor of Salisbury, England, as Salisbury kicked off its Bicentennial Celebration in 1932. *Poplar Hill Collection.*

Opposite, top: This is the colorful program for Salisbury's Bicentennial Celebration in 1932, produced by the Ulman Theatre. *Poplar Hill Collection.*

Opposite, bottom: Salisburians competed in numerous events. Here we see a shot from the 1940 Fourth of July celebration and soapbox derby as a lone contestant rolls down East Main Street past the city park. *Salisbury Chamber of Commerce Collection.*

THE SPIRIT OF '76
ULMAN'S THEATRE
PROGRAM
BICENTENNIAL WEEK
AUGUST 8-13

This massive nurses' float was part of the 1932 bicentennial parade. *Poplar Hill Collection.*

Salisbury was portrayed in many ways in the 1932 celebration. First, we see the Sportsman's Paradise float. *Poplar Hill Collection.*

Margaret Laws sits high on this float representing the Spirit of Agriculture in 1932. *Poplar Hill Collection.*

Adele Dolby rests on a pile of silver dollars, demonstrating Salisbury's Financial Strength of 1932. *Poplar Hill Collection.*

Betty Allen sits in the Heart of the Land of Evergreens on this 1932 float. *Poplar Hill Collection.*

Athletes and swimmers give a sampling of recreation in Salisbury in 1932. *Poplar Hill Collection.*

Girls show off the various tasks of Dairying on this 1932 float. *Poplar Hill Collection.*

The four girls on this float appear to be enjoying the fruits of Prosperity in 1932. *Poplar Hill Collection.*

Finally, here is the queen herself, Carolyn Waller, along with her court, to wrap up this sampling of bicentennial activities. Carolyn lived to see the Sesquibicentennial of 1982. *Poplar Hill Collection.*

Salisbury again came to life in 1982 to celebrate 250 years of existence. Dressed in colonial-era finery are the Paddleboat Belles down at the park. *Barbara Wimbrow White Collection.*

Shown here are the Paddleboat Brothers of the 1982 celebration. *Barbara Wimbrow White Collection.*

Transportation

Movin' on Up

The Wicomico River served as the main conveyance of people and goods such as produce, seafood, grain, fuel oil and fertilizers. The steamship *Patuxent* regularly sailed until the Wicomico River's shallowness demanded dredging.

Salisbury's history of transportation is checkered. From pedestrian paths to stagecoach lanes, scowls, steamboats, rail, freighters and barges, vehicles and, lastly, airplanes, Salisbury is the economic focus of Delmarva.

Steamboating began in 1830. The Wicomico River's active seaport is the second busiest port in the state. Steady steamboat service began with the *Kent* in 1855, and then the *Virginia*, which ran for twenty-one years. The grand paddleboats ceased nearly one hundred years later, circa 1929, after the introduction of the Eastern Shore Railway in 1853. Eventually, powerboats, ferries, passenger ships and barges were common modes of transference. The Civil War interrupted the progress of rail. But by 1906, the horseless carriage began its evolution into the modern vehicle.

By 1901, trains consisted of refrigerator cars that blessed the growers and the travelers who fell into the rhythm of shuffling rail and steamers. Union Station, constructed in 1914, terminated in Salisbury, making the city a boomtown. Elsbeth Mantler notes that in 1906 R.L. Hoxie, lieutenant colonel of the U.S. Army Corps of Engineers, stated that "Salisbury…is a town of increasing importance, having a present commerce of considerable value, with excellent prospect of continued commercial expansion in the future." By 1949, diesel engines had come online, but nine years later, rail dissolved even though barges swept the river; city leaders had chosen to support oyster shell road building rather than railroading.

Buses grew in popularity (Red Star, Trailways and now Greyhound) until aviation finally took off. So this "new official port of Salisbury in 1732 gradually became a gateway to an ever-spreading area of colonists seeking more land for homesteading," according to the website for the City of Salisbury, Maryland. Chesapeake Airways originated in 1946 and ceased in 1949; then came philanthropist Richard Henson's airlines in 1967, which later became Piedmont Airlines, a U.S. Airways holding. Air traffic skyrocketed in and out of the circa 1947 Wicomico County Regional Airport. A new, larger airport was built in 1990 and retitled the Salisbury–Ocean City Airport, and like Salisbury's marina, its airport is also second in the state, transporting about 135,000 passengers annually, propelling Salisbury into the twenty-first century.

Shore Transit—the region's mass transportation system—soon came on the scene, traveling about nine routes daily throughout not only Salisbury and Wicomico County, but also Ocean City, Princess Anne and Somerset. The transit authority recently purchased seven additional buses and has over one hundred drivers, noted Salisbury Chamber of Commerce executive director Brad Bellacicco. Greyhound bus service is looking to share a new terminal with ShoreTran.

Dan Landsman notes in "The Heart of Salisbury" that "[n]ow, with transportation opened north in addition to west, Salisbury became the middleman between Baltimore and Wilmington and Philadelphia and later, Norfolk." The City of Salisbury proudly remarks, "[This] once small colonial outpost…is now one of Maryland's most progressive and respected communities preparing to continue its heritage."

River commerce remains an important facet of Salisbury industry as this barge is gently pushed along toward Salisbury docks. *Wicomico County Historical Society Collection.*

Shown here is the *Kent*, one of the first steamboats to travel the Wicomico. Its run in 1855 was short, and for a time Salisbury had no steamboat service. *John E. Jacob Collection.*

Salisbury was served for years by the steamship *Victor Lynn*, seen here in 1937. *Enoch Pratt Free Library Collection.*

This old photo shows the rail line going through Salisbury about 1905. The line benefitted from a new station in 1914. *George Chevallier Collection.*

In the first half of the twentieth century, engines like this E3 model regularly passed through Salisbury's Union Station. This train is on its way from Delmar, just a few miles north of Salisbury. *Hilda Fowler Collection.*

This overhead shot was taken in 1908 and shows the Baltimore Chesapeake and Atlantic Freight Line track heading past Salisbury. Toward the top you can see part of its line that ran across Johnson's lake. *Edward H. Nabb Research Center for Delmarva History and Culture at Salisbury University and the Wicomico Historical Society Collection.*

Salisbury Marine Railway Company opened in 1901 after Otis Lloyd purchased the shipyard and operated briskly through two world wars. *John E. Jacob Collection.*

Regular bus service in Salisbury was handled by the Red Star Motorcoach Company, beginning in 1926, followed eventually by Carolina Trailways in 1952. Today, Salisburians leave the driving to Greyhound. The station moved to Cypress Street and currently is looking for a new Salisbury location. *John E. Jacob Collection.*

This colorful postcard shows a transport from Chesapeake Airways flying over Salisbury. Regular service to Baltimore was instituted from 1946 until 1949. The original terminal has changed hands several times over the years. Today, small airlines soar to not only Baltimore and D.C., but also to Philadelphia; Norfolk; Charlotte, North Carolina; and other jump-off places. Airport runways are undergoing expansion to accommodate jets. The Salisbury airport handled 116,705 passengers in 2008 on in-coming and out-going flights. *Martha Graham Collection.*

This rustic old Texaco Station once stood at the corner of Main and Church Streets about where the current Thirsty's convenience store sits. *George Chevallier Collection.*

Worship

"Let Us Bow in Prayer"

Salisbury's religious roots are complicated. In the 1600s, the pioneers came face to face with the Nanticoke Indians, who did not share the same devotion.

The colonists' Puritanism and Anglicanism served as a community magnet and a place for recreation, family bonding and worship. The many Puritans empowered the colonists to initiate the Maryland Toleration Act in 1649, which encouraged tolerance of others' beliefs (as long as they were Christian); yet this act sentenced anyone to death who denied the divinity of Jesus. Oliver Cromwell revoked it.

As Richard W. Cooper noted in *Portrait of Salisbury, Maryland thru the 1990s*, "[From the] 1692 Act of Establishment…the Anglican or the Church of England…require[d] the citizenry…to pay stipulated church dues regardless of what their persuasion may be."

Anglicans, Presbyterians and Baptists appeared, followed by Methodism, which took root for the next generation. Baptists and Methodists split into other groups. Meanwhile, Catholics and Lutherans punched their way into the area. Though small in number, Jews rented space until 1951. Their synagogue, Beth Israel, was founded in 1925 and is now located on Camden and Winder Streets.

Today, nearly every religion is represented in the Salisbury area, including not only Christian variants but also those of Hindu, Islam, Jewish, Scientologist, Mormon, Seventh-Day Adventist, Jehovah Witness, Unitarian Universalist and other interdenominational faiths.

In this 1904 photo, Pilgrim Holiness Church is standing where the Salvation Army Thrift Store on Eastern Shore Drive serves the community. *George Chevallier Collection.*

Known popularly as the Old Synagogue Building, this edifice still stands at the southwest corner of Main and Market Streets, as seen in this 1896 engraving. For years, it was occupied by a variety of downstairs shops, while the congregation met upstairs. *John E. Jacob Collection.*

An 1845 engraving shows St. Peter's Episcopal Church before it was nearly destroyed by two devastating fires in the last half of the same century. *John E. Jacob Collection.*

Though its steeple has been altered from this 1908 photo, the Wicomico Presbyterian Church still stands along Church Street. *Edward H. Nabb Research Center for Delmarva History and Culture at Salisbury University and the Wicomico Historical Society Collection.*

Opposite, top: This 1930s photo shows the same St. Peter's Church as it looks today. Notice the truncated bell tower and altered front doorway area. *George Chevallier Collection.*

Opposite, bottom: In 1908, the Division Street Baptist Church had a modest congregation, but over time it became the Allen Memorial Baptist Church and outgrew this location. *Edward H. Nabb Research Center for Delmarva History and Culture at Salisbury University and the Wicomico Historical Society Collection.*

Established in 1884, St. Paul AME Zion Church, seen here in 1908, had just undergone remodeling at its Church Street location. The building now houses the Chipman Cultural Center. *Edward H. Nabb Research Center for Delmarva History and Culture at Salisbury University and the Wicomico Historical Society Collection.*

Opposite, top: Trinity United Methodist Church was built as a result of a huge fund drive by its congregation, which included ex-governor E.E. Jackson as its principal benefactor, and still stands near North Division Street. *Salisbury Chamber of Commerce Collection.*

Opposite, bottom: St. Francis de Sales Catholic Church—with about four thousand families as members—moved from its downtown location in 1964 to its present Riverside Drive site. Behind it, facing Camden Avenue, was its religious school, seen here. It recently completed a large addition to the school. *Salisbury Chamber of Commerce Collection.*

Asbury United Methodist Church remains one of the largest churches of its denomination in the area. Though the congregation dates back to the 1700s, the present building was constructed in 1964. *George Chevallier Collection.*

Established in 1996 to meet the needs of an exploding Moslem population, the Islamic Society of America serves nearly two hundred members from its location along Jersey Road. *Authors' Collection.*

The First Church of Christ, Scientist, moved into this location on South Boulevard and Smith Street in 1949, not long before this photo was taken. It is still there. *Salisbury Chamber of Commerce Collection.*

Healthcare

More than a Band-Aid Fix

When ill or injured, colonists relied on others to perform magical, mystical and herbal healing until doctors appeared and did house calls. Hunter Mann III says, "Whenever my grandfather made house calls, his dog would sit on the car's running board, never jumping off while it was moving." Medicine back then was archaic—partly knowledge, partly guesswork and partly luck.

Today, titan Peninsula Regional Medical Center (PRMC) is a dazzling, state-of-the-art, high-tech facility. Its humble beginning was launched as Peninsula General Hospital (PGH), located in two houses on the corner of West Main and Fitzwater Streets. It is a boon to Salisburians and those in the 350,000 service metro belt, ranking in the top one hundred hospitals nationally in cardiac, cancer, orthopedics, GI, neonatal, pulmonary and trauma care. It leads hospitals in laparoscopic and robotic surgery, and in some departments, it ranks in the top five.

Unprecedented growth and its immense size would have amazed its founders, Drs. Todd and Dick, with its "330 physicians, and 3000 employees who treat over 500,000 people each year." PRMC also leads national hospitals with a "$100 million expansion, with 220,000 square feet of new space; 80,000 additional square feet of existing space will be redesigned," according to its biographical information online. This colossal hospital has six main entrances.

Pine Bluff Hospital was established in 1912 as a private institution until the state reinitiated it in 1950 as a sanatorium for twenty-four tuberculosis patients. It has changed focus over the years; today, it's a center for senior citizens.

Deer's Head Hospital opened in 1950 for chronic diseases; it remains in operation. Three nursing homes—providing over five hundred beds—cover Salisbury's elderly and rehabilitative patients: Wicomico Nursing Home, initiated by Agatha Polk; Salisbury Center on Civic Avenue; and Anchorage Nursing and Rehabilitation Center at Times Square. River Walk Manor, Parson's Home and other medical institutes, such as HealthSouth Chesapeake Rehabilitation Hospital, dot the landscape. Clinics, healthcare and urgent care centers, hospices and assisted living quarters also offer treatment.

Salisbury has earned accolades for providing the best medical care on the Eastern Shore.

Salisbury's original hospital was opened in 1897 by Dr. George W. Todd, who converted two houses on Fitzwater Street. *John E. Jacob Collection.*

In 1898, Dr. James MacFaddin Dick came onboard as a surgeon and worked at the hospital until his death in 1939. *John E. Jacob Collection.*

Shortly after the new hospital was built, Helen Wise opened a nursing school at the hospital and, in 1905, moved it to a permanent building. *Peninsula Regional Medical Center Collection.*

The hospital's horse-drawn ambulance was replaced in 1919 by a motorized version, seen here about 1925. *Peninsula Regional Medical Center Collection.*

This photo shows Dr. Hunter Mann making his rounds, with his faithful dog on the running board of his roadster sometime about 1934. The days of doctors making house calls are long gone. *Hunter Mann III Collection.*

Opposite, top: This photo shows the graduating class of 1908 from the newly built school. *Peninsula Regional Medical Center Collection.*

Opposite, middle: The hospital moved into a new facility in 1904, thanks to a donation of $50,000 by William H. Jackson. This photo dates to 1907. *George Chevallier Collection.*

Opposite, bottom: This circa 1950 photo shows the hospital at the midpoint of its phenomenal growth as a fire drill takes place. *Salisbury Chamber of Commerce Collection.*

The home of Humphrey Humphreys on Broad Street was turned into a therapeutic institute by his son, Dr. Eugene Humphreys, after his father's death in 1882. *John E. Jacob Collection.*

Dr. George Todd also initiated what became Pine Bluff Sanatorium in 1909 for the treatment of tuberculosis. It was later purchased by the state and now serves as a residence and facility for the elderly. *Martha Graham Collection.*

Deer's Head State Hospital opened in 1950 to perform rehabilitation of long-term illnesses, and it sits on the north side of town. *Salisbury Chamber of Commerce Collection.*

The John B. Parsons Home for the Aged, shown in this 1936 photo, was built atop Lemmon Hill with money from his estate. He also put $1 million aside to be held in trust. Parson's Home still exists. *Enoch Pratt Free Library Collection.*

Education

Life Lessons and Book Learnin'

The colonists relied on individual or group tutoring by family members, clergy or indentured servants. Wealthy children went to boarding schools elsewhere—even to England—but parents desired a closer institution, so they opened academies with donations from the public, businesses and the state. In 1818, boys attended Salisbury Academy; girls had to wait five more years to be admitted. Public schools emerged in 1885 and progressed to eighty-eight schools in 1903, says Charles J. Truitt in *Historic Salisbury Updated: 1662–1982*.

Boys studied "orthography, Latin, Greek, geography, logistics, navigation, surveying, oratory, mathematics and philosophy" while girls learned "housewifery, domestic chores, and…social etiquette," noted Truitt. Parents purchased textbooks and helped construct austere one-room schools with clapboard siding and potbellied stoves. Teachers—not much older than ages seventeen to twenty-two—sat at desks on raised platforms, earning about ninety dollars per term for fifteen students.

About 1896, all one-room schools were replaced with two-story buildings. Segregation and parochial institutions advanced. "Mardela High School is the only high school left outside of Salisbury," says John E. Jacob in *Salisbury in Vintage Postcards*.

Middle schools were added and additions tacked on. County education today has grown to "25 schools, and 14,633 students, consisting of 16 elementary schools, 1 elementary/middle school, 3 middle schools, 1 middle/high school, and 4 high schools, including Evening High School.

Approximately 3,000 employees work for the school system," according to the Wicomico County Public Schools website, so it ranks in size with city/county government, the hospital and university employees.

A new Bennett high school is being built for $73 million to help accommodate all the new "Come Heres." There are numerous private and preparatory schools.

Since 1925, Salisbury Normal School has undergone various name changes to emerge as Salisbury University with about eight thousand students and a respected reputation. In 1975, Wor-Wic Technical Community College opened and now instructs over eleven thousand students. It, too, has undergone modifications and a name change to Wor-Wic Community College.

Eastern Shore College closed in 1964. Defunct Jefferson School of Commerce—chartered 1960—taught bookkeeping, shorthand, accounting and business math. PRMC (then PGH) had a nursing school in 1905. A branch of Sojourner Douglass College opened in Salisbury in 1994.

Salisbury equals quality education.

When this photo was taken in 1908, the Eastern Shore College had been around for four years and was Salisbury's first business school. *Edward H. Nabb Research Center for Delmarva History and Culture at Salisbury University and the Wicomico Historical Society Collection.*

Salisbury Academy opened in 1818 along Division and Chestnut Streets and is seen here about 1850. It remained a private academy but burned down in the Great Fire of 1886. *John E. Jacob Collection.*

As noted earlier, sports were always part of education in Salisbury. Here is the 1904 Wicomico High School football team. *John E. Jacob Collection.*

Before racial integration, most counties provided "separate but equal" facilities, as shown here by this all–African American science class from Salisbury High School in 1961. *John E. Jacob Collection.*

Opposite, top: Even though the Salisbury Academy burned down in 1886, education continued on Chestnut Street, as seen here in this 1909 photograph of the Chestnut Street school. *George Chevallier Collection.*

Opposite, middle: Prior to the new school being built in 1931, Wicomico County's only high school sat on Upton Street overlooking Humphreys Lake and only went up to the tenth grade when this photo was taken circa 1905. *John E. Jacob Collection.*

Charles H. Chipman remains the most beloved African American educator in Salisbury. Starting in 1915 as principal of the Salisbury Elementary and Salisbury Industrial School, he served in many positions until his retirement in 1961 and is credited with helping to calm racial tensions during the turbulent 1960s. *John E. Jacob Collection.*

Above: Salisbury Normal School started as a teachers' college in 1925, and Holloway Hall was its only building, as seen in this 1940s photo. Now called Salisbury University, it covers 155 acres and educates almost eight thousand students. *Martha Graham Collection.*

Below: Jefferson School of Commerce started in 1959 with fourteen students and two teachers. By 1963, it had grown considerably. *Jefferson School yearbook photo.*

East Salisbury Elementary School students are seen here in this 1947 photo. The school still stands on Old Ocean City Road. *George Chevallier Collection.*

To meet further demand, Parkside High School was opened in 1975 on Beaglin Park Drive and served over 1,200 students. It underwent major renovations in 1997 and houses the county's only planetarium. *Authors' Collection.*

Opposite, bottom: Wor-Wic Technical Community College started in 1975 by offering evening courses in far-flung classrooms across the two counties of Worcester and Wicomico before it was consolidated into a beautiful campus on Campus Drive in 1989; it also serves Somerset County. Its name changed simply to Wor-Wic Community College. *Authors' Collection.*

James M. Bennett Senior High School was built in 1962 and was rebuilt on another part of the same property, greatly expanded and having a student population exceeding 1,300 as of 2008. *Authors' Collection*.

Disasters

Woe Is I

The imposing geographical location of the Eastern Shore promotes weather that prompts catastrophic storms, from nor'easters to roaring thunderstorms. Hurricane Hazel tore up much of the area, destroying businesses and other structures, felling trees and cutting power.

Salisburians also dealt with other major cataclysms—fires, flooding, high tides, thick fogs, train wrecks, industrial explosions, shipwrecks and other misfortunes.

The foremost conflagration in 1860 paled in comparison to the 1886 Great Fire. Twenty-two acres of the business center and churches burned, charring the St. Peter's Church bell. Damage totaled nearly $1 million.

Other fires bucked up, taking out such businesses as the Jackson Ice Plant, the armory, Kennerly, the civic center, the Ulman Theatre and Wimbrow Machine Shop. "Due to devastating nineteenth century fires, no building from this period survives in modern day Salisbury," says Paul Baker Touart in *At the Crossroads*.

On May 28, 1909, at 2:00 p.m., the Humphreys Dam break completely emptied its lake.

This chapter highlights the colonists' hardships, from Mother Nature to human error.

The Great Fire occurred on Sunday, October 17, 1886, but another fire nearing the extent of the 1886 conflagration had torched four business blocks of the city in 1860. It started at Daniel Davis's frame building on the corner of St. Peter's and Main Streets. Though the 1860 fire was not as bad as the 1886 fire, it still left its footprint for years to come. Ironically, the water pumper was burned in the fire. *Hunter Mann III Collection.*

The 1886 fire destroyed most of the city. The steam engine and hose carriages wouldn't work, so the small blaze turned into a heart-wrenching conflagration. *John E. Jacob Collection.*

A bucket brigade went into motion to extinguish the inferno, but it was a futile act, and the brigade was pulled back from the intense heat. *Salisbury Chamber of Commerce Collection.*

In less than four hours, twenty-two acres of the city had been burned. At least 209 buildings were in ashes. *Hunter Mann III Collection.*

This bell at St. Peter's Church tolled for the 1886 fire and melted an hour later. Though the Catholic church was the first to succumb, Asbury Methodist Church was the last to go. *Hunter Mann III Collection.*

Jackson Ice Plant opened in 1901 with a thirty-cubic-foot storage room. This photo shows the July 1907 fire, with damages totaling about $10,000. *George Chevallier Collection.*

Some lumberyards and mills opened as early as 1743 with the construction of Humphreys Dam. The dam split the Wicomico River into east and west sides. On May 28, 1909, about 2:00 p.m., the dam collapsed, blamed on the excessive weight on South Division Street. The lake water rushed down the Wicomico, destroying boats, mills and everything else in its path. *John E. Jacob Collection.*

The dam breaking changed downtown forever, opening up more land for commercial development. *John E. Jacob Collection.*

On June 26, 1915, the repair shop at the BC&A Railroad caught fire. By a miracle, nobody was killed and nearby property was saved. *John E. Jacob Collection.*

The Salisbury Milling Company's flour mills burned down. *John E. Jacob Collection.*

The old armory on West Church Street burned down in 1914 not long after the new one was built. *John E. Jacob Collection.*

The Peninsula Hotel burned down in January 1929, and its location on the corner of St. Peter's and Main Streets is now occupied by the AllFirst Bank. *George Chevallier Collection.*

In May 1944, a fire snuffed out the Kennerly Building, just one of three fires to hit downtown in the 1940s. It was not rebuilt. *John E. Jacob Collection.*

Opposite, top: Hurricane Hazel hit Maryland in 1954 right between the eyes. Not the first of many storms, this one carried gusts nearly one hundred miles per hour and heavy rains. This shows just a fraction of the damage to Salisbury. Overall damage totaled about $10 million. *John E. Jacob Collection.*

Oppoosite, bottom: Firefighter Hunter Mann III recalls that frigid, icy Saturday in the early 1960s when the Ulman Theatre fire started and how the freezing day prevented water from coming out of the fire hydrants. *John E. Jacob Collection.*

ULMAN
"AROUND THE
WORLD IN A DAZE"
BIG BEAT

On October 7, 1972, on C. Ercel Wimbrow's seventy-third birthday, one hundred firemen battled the four-hour blaze at his machine shop. Damages came in at about $100,000, but he was back in business three weeks later. *Barbara Wimbrow White Collection.*

In June 1977, 100 people were inside the circa 1959 civic center. Mostly kids, they were attending an arts and crafts workshop. A spark from a floor finish stripper ignited the wooden floor. Over 180 men and thirty pieces of apparatus fought to put it out. Damages exceeded $4 million. *Hunter Mann III Collection.*

Growth

Expansion in All Directions

We opened this book discussing the growth of Salisbury from its early existence as part of old Somerset to its current condition of prosperity—big city retail, high-tech jobs, major industries, top-notch medical care, ease of transportation, excellence in education and a church for every soul. So now we close this book with growth, as well.

You can envision in the olden days women with their bonnets, dresses covered by aprons, holding kids' hands as they amble down Main Street and pop in to talk to merchants; you can envision the early hour when they rise and toil, with dad in bib overalls and wearing a hat to block the sun; you can envision the dark nights at home with the family bowing their heads in prayer before eating a simple dinner and then—Walton family style—bidding each other "Goodnight, John Boy."

From the one-horse buggy paths to dirt back roads to oyster shell streets, Salisbury leaves behind the quaintness of a small town where everybody knew everybody and colonists all went to the general store to shop and talk. Today, the little town is a metropolis—where you can go to the same grocery store every week and not know anyone; where planes and expensive cars substitute for stagecoaches; where big box stores replace soda fountains and luncheonettes; where mega-churches overcome prayerful groups meeting in homes; and where mail by horseback is replaced by e-mail.

If living back in eras past, you would have been eager to see William Humphreys Jackson, Maryland congressman in the early 1900s, or Elihu Jackson, governor from 1888 to 1892 and key player in Salisbury's history.

Others who have visited, performed in, moved to or were born in Salisbury include Franklin Delano Roosevelt; actors Dale Midkiff, John Glover and Linda Hamilton; Senator Paul Sarbanes; national meteorologist Mike Seidel; Tom Brown, Green Bay Packers player and Senators' baseball player; Barrie Tilghman, first female mayor of Salisbury; swimmer Michael Phelps; Michelle Obama; Charlie Daniels and band; Lynyrd Skynyrd band; Fernando Guerrero, Salisbury's homegrown professional boxer; and other distinguished figures who have visited and been invited by local universities.

Just as the beloved Salisbury of the early years drew people to it, the Salisbury of modern day embraces and pulls them in.

The seventy-year-old Junior Chamber of Commerce initiated the celebration of Salisbury's 275th anniversary. *From left*: JC president David Smith; noted historian and JC founding president John E. Jacob, who chaired the local U.S. Bicentennial Celebration; and former JC president Mathew Alexander. *Jason Rhodes Collection.*

Opposite, top: Cakes by Sylvia spent time recreating Salisbury's first city hall for the 275th celebration. *Jason Rhodes Collection.*

Opposite, bottom: Local morning anchor Jimmy Hoppa is shown emceeing the 275th celebration. *Jason Rhodes Collection.*

Happy 275th anniversary
Salisbury

EXIT
275 YEARS Happy Anniversary
SALISBURY

Other attendees at the 275th celebration are, *from left*, Jennifer Garden, Salisbury University (SU) student; Pat Taylor of Wicomico Historical Commission and Edward H. Nabb Research Center for Delmarva History and Culture at SU Board of Directors; Dr. G. Ray Thompson, director of the Nabb Center; and Jason Rhodes, the 275th anniversary celebration chairman. *Jason Rhodes Collection.*

The first major shopping center was the Salisbury Mall, which declined after a large new mall—called The Centre at Salisbury—opened on the north side in 1990. The old mall was razed, the pile of rubble now gone. This was one of the last photos of it still standing. What to do with the old mall became a mantra of city council and residents, who couldn't agree on the perfect replacement; it now showcases acres of flat, vacant land while the debate continues. *Authors' Collection.*

The Lord Salisbury Motel was a lodging staple until it was torn down to make way for what is now a shopping center full of big box stores, such as Bed, Bath and Beyond; Old Navy; and other major retail stores. *George Chevallier Collection.*

This section of downtown has seen its problems, from being the main street of activity to cobblestoning it and closing it off to traffic as a pedestrian mall and then to reopening it for one-way traffic. Retail in the North Corridor took a bite out of foot traffic downtown. *Authors' Collection.*

The Boulevard Theatre was built in 1948 with Art Deco styling, and by 1980, it was the only theatre left downtown. *Authors' Collection.*

In 1990, Regal Theatres donated the Boulevard to the Salisbury Wicomico Arts Council, which couldn't find funding to renovate it. It was purchased by a local businessman and razed, and it is now an empty lot. *Authors' Collection.*

This is the new Station 16, headquarters of the Salisbury Fire Department. This huge building sits off Cypress Street and houses its museum, state-of-the-art firefighting equipment, cooking facilities and dorms for student firefighters. *Authors' Collection.*

This was the old fire department headquarters, built in 1928 across from what was then the armory (now that building is the Wicomico library). This building is no longer in use, as it has been replaced by the new firehouse on Cypress Street. *Authors' Collection.*

ONE WAY
DO NOT
ENTER

Bibliography

Bellacicco, Brad, Executive Director. Salisbury Chamber of Commerce. Personal correspondence with authors.

"Colonial Maryland" blog. http://colonialmaryland.blogspot.com.

Cooper, Rachel. "Maryland's Eastern Shore: A Visitors Guide to the Eastern Shore of Maryland." About.com. http://dc.about.com/od/daytripsgetaways/a/EasternShore.htm.

Cooper, Richard W. "History and Facts of Salisbury MD—The Crossroads of Delmarva." City of Salisbury, Maryland, 1999. http://www.ci.salisbury.md.us/Home/HistoryandFacts/tabid/541/Default.aspx.

———. "Imagining Life Here in the 1600s." *Portrait of Salisbury, Maryland through the 1900s*. Baltimore, MD: Gateway Press, Inc., 1994.

Corddry, George H. *Wicomico County History*. Maryland: Peninsula Press, 1981.

Jacob, John E. "Education." Chap. 11 in *Salisbury in Vintage Postcards*. Charleston, SC: Arcadia Publishing, 1998.

———. *Salisbury and Wicomico County: A Pictorial History*. Virginia Beach, VA: Donning Company Publishers, 1981.

Landsman, Dan. "The Heart of Salisbury." Chap. 2 in "Exploring the Chesapeake's Forgotten River: Perspectives on the Wicomico." http://faculty.salisbury.edu/~mllewis/wicomico_river/chapter_two.htm.

Mann, Hunter. Personal correspondence with authors, June 2009.

Mantler, Elsbeth. "Chapter Two: Agriculture in Wicomico County prior to 1880." Salisbury University. http://faculty.salisbury.edu/~mllewis/Agriculture/chapter_two_introduction.htm.

Nabb Research Center Resources. "January 9, 2006—Somerset County Farming—Then and Now." Pamphlet, 1905.

Peninsula Regional Medical Center. "About Us." http://www.peninsula.org/body.cfm?id=20.

"Salisbury, Maryland." Economy and Businesses section. Wikipedia, the free encyclopedia. http://en.wikipedia.org/wiki/Salisbury,_MD#Economy_and_businesses.

Touart, Paul Baker. "Bounded by the Wicomico, Nanticoke and Pocomoke 1750–1820." Chap. 3 in *At the Crossroads: The Architectural History of Wicomico, Maryland.* Wicomico County, MD: Preservation Trust of Wicomico County, 2009.

TripCart Beta. "Local Flavor on the Delmarva Peninsula." Eastern North Carolina, Virginia and Maryland. http://www.tripcart.com/usa-regions/Eastern-North-Carolina-Virginia-Maryland,Society-Culture.aspx.

Truitt, Charles J. *Historic Salisbury Updated: 1662–1982.* Salisbury, MD: Historical Books, Inc., 1982.

Wicomico County Public Schools. "Profile." http://www.wcboe.org/boe/documents/School_Profile.

About the Authors

Dr. Gianni DeVincenti Hayes has been writing and speaking professionally for twenty-five years. She earned her PhD *summa cum laude* in English, writing and comparative literature, as well as two master's degrees, a bachelor's degree and certification in writing from University of Rochester and Middlebury College. She's been honored with the Distinguished Alumni Award from both her high school and college. She's a former college department chair and professor, author of seventeen published books and hundreds of stories for national magazines. She's an online syndicated columnist for twenty-four publications, and she hosts an international radio talk show, as well as local TV and radio shows. She founded the Writers Bloc, Inc. The University of Maryland system set up an archive in her name for the collection of her writings. She has appeared on *A&E Biography* and Pennsylvania cable network TV comprising 145 stations statewide. She is married and has two daughters.

Andy Nunez has spent his entire life on the Eastern Shore of Maryland and is the author of several books on local life and folklore. He has earned his bachelor's degree from the University of Maryland Eastern Shore and lives in Salisbury with his wife and family. Currently he is the vice-president of the Writers Bloc, Inc., of the Eastern Shore. This is his sixth book. He is also a local TV and radio host for public access television.